Maths Around Us

Sorting at the Market

Tracey Steffora

www.raintreepublishers.co.uk
Visit our website to find out more information about Raintree books.

To order:
☎ Phone 0845 6044371
▭ Fax +44 (0) 1865 312263
▭ Email myorders@raintreepublishers.co.uk

Customers from outside the UK please telephone +44 1865 312262

Raintree is an imprint of Capstone Global Library Limited, a company incorporated in England and Wales having its registered office at 7 Pilgrim Street, London, EC4V 6LB – Registered company number: 6695582

Edited by Rebecca Rissman, Tracey Steffora, and Catherine Veitch
Designed by Joanna Hinton-Malivoire
Picture research by Elizabeth Alexander
Production by Victoria Fitzgerald
Originated by Capstone Global Library Ltd
Printed and bound in China by Leo Paper Products Ltd

ISBN 978 1 406 22320 0
15 14 13 12 11
10 9 8 7 6 5 4 3 2 1

British Library Cataloguing in Publication Data
Steffora, Tracey.
Sorting at the market. -- (Maths around us)
511.3'22-dc22

Acknowledgements
The author and publisher are grateful to the following for permission to reproduce photographs: © Capstone Publishers pp. 11, 12, 15, 16, 19, 20 (Karon Dubke); Alamy pp. 17 (© DC Premiumstock), 18 (© Wiskerke), 21 (© ephotocorp), 23 glossary – lantern (© ephotocorp); Corbis p. 7 (© Brigitte Sporrer); iStockphoto pp. 9, 23 – glossary bin (© Stephanie DeLay); Photolibrary pp. 10 (Martin Siepmann/imagebroker), 14 (Egmont Strigl/imagebroker); Shutterstock pp. 4 (© Tupungato), 5 (© hpf), 8 (© Manuel Fernandes), 13 (© Andre Nantel), 22 (© Sia Chen How).

Cover photograph of a fruit market reproduced with permission of Shutterstock (© Manuel Fernandes). Back cover photograph of a flower market in Montreal reproduced with permission of Shutterstock (© Andre Nantel).

We would like to thank Nancy Harris, Dee Reid, and Diana Bentley for their assistance in the preparation of this book.

Contents

At the market

We sort things every day.

There are many ways to sort things
at the market.

Shopping list

vegetables	fruit
potatoes	bananas
carrots	strawberries
green beans	grapes

We sort things on a list.

We sort things in bags.

We sort things in baskets.

recycle

rubbish

We sort things in bins.

Colour

We sort things by colour.

How would you sort these peppers?

Some are yellow. Some are green.
Some are red.

These flowers are sorted by colour.

Size

We sort things by size.

How would you sort these tomatoes?

Some are big. Some are small.

These hats are sorted by size.

Shape

We sort things by shape.

How would you sort this bread?

oval

round

Some are round. Some are oval.
Some are long and thin.

20

These lanterns are sorted by shape.

Sorting all around

There are things to sort everywhere!

How can you sort things?

Picture glossary

 **bin** container that holds rubbish or recycling

 **lantern** type of light

Index

Notes for parents and teachers

Before reading

Being able to classify and group items into a set is an important mathematical concept
for children to acquire. Prepare a selection of circles, squares, and triangles of various colours
and have each child choose one out of a bowl. Ask all children holding triangles to stand in
one group, all those holding squares in another group, and all those holding circles in a third
group. Explain that the objects have just been sorted by shape. Have all the children come back
together and ask them to get into groups by colour. Explain that when we sort objects, we are
finding something that is alike about them and putting them
in groups.

After reading

Extend children's understanding of fruits and vegetables by explaining that fruits are the
part of the plant that contains seeds, and vegetables are other plant parts that we eat
(e.g. roots, leaves, stems). With children, review the list on page 6 and discuss other fruits and
vegetables that can be added to each category of the list. If possible, provide actual examples
or photos of the items. You might even have children sort the objects further (green vegetables,
orange vegetables, red fruits, etc.).